WORDS FOR WRITING

Katy Pike

Contents

Pirates

Pirates are the robbers of the sea. They travel the seas stealing from other boats and ships.

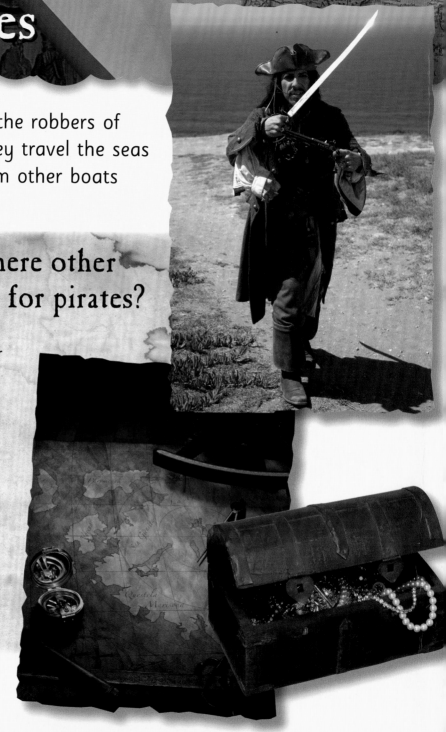

Are there other words for pirates?

nouns
adventurer
buccaneer
freebooter
marauder
picaroon
plunderer
raider
robber
rogue
sea dog
sea wolf
thief

How could you describe your pirate?

Blackbeard's hair was as wild as his temper. Smoke crept from under his hat as if his head was on fire. When he boarded a ship, he carried a sharpened cutlass and various guns and knives.

Is your pirate silly or cruel?

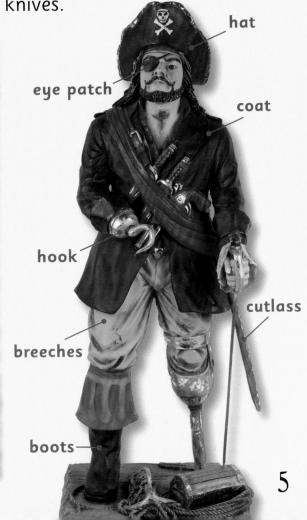

hat

eye patch

coat

hook

cutlass

breeches

boots

silly words	cruel words
amusing	aggressive
clever	bloodthirsty
funny	bold
hilarious	cutthroat
humorous	ferocious
mysterious	fierce
one-eyed	merciless
reckless	nasty
side-splitting	ruthless
spirited	savage
strange	vicious
weird	violent
zany	wicked

What do pirates wear?

The pirate's breeches were torn and fraying at the knees. Her long, red hair spilled out from under her woollen headscarf. She shivered as the wind whipped through her threadbare cloak. The boat rocked and creaked through the storm.

nouns	adjectives
belt	black
boots	bleached
breeches	colorful
buckles	drab
cloak	filthy
cutlass	leather
earring	old
eye patch	patched
headscarf	salty
hat	stained
hook	tattered
sash	threadbare
	torn

What do pirates do?

The pirates bombarded ships with cannon fire. They tossed grappling hooks and boarded ships. They fought the soldiers and looted all the cabins.

How did they speak?

barked	howled	stuttered
bellowed	laughed	uttered
blurted	roared	whispered
cackled	screamed	whooped
called	shouted	yelled
chuckled	shrieked	
cried		
declared		
giggled		
hooted		

verbs

aimed	clashed
attacked	fought
battered	gave up
battled	grappled
boarded	looted
bombarded	plundered
burned	pounded
	sank
	shook
	struggled
	tossed
	wounded

What if ...

You are a stowaway on a sailing ship that is taken over by pirates. Would you fight them or join them? You need to be brave and smart and ...

Ships and Boats

Captain Blackheart and his crew set sail on an ancient clipper — she was old but she was fast. These well-armed pirates were hunting for treasure. They'd heard that a gold-filled galleon was just off the coast. They planned to attack at dawn, taking everything — ship, crew, and all.

ferry

sailboat

What type of boat will your pirates use?

nouns

banana boat	houseboat
battle cruiser	lifeboat
canoe	outrigger
cargo ship	paddleboat
catamaran	powerboat
clipper	rowboat
dinghy	sailboat
felucca	schooner
ferry	skiff
frigate	submarine
galleon	tanker
galley	

submarine

catamaran

powerboat

clipper

tugboat

Parts of a ship

nouns

boom	gangplank	propeller
bow	gunwales	oars
bridge	hull	rigging
bulkhead	keel	rudder
cargo hold	lookout	sail
deck	mast	stern
galley	porthole	wheel

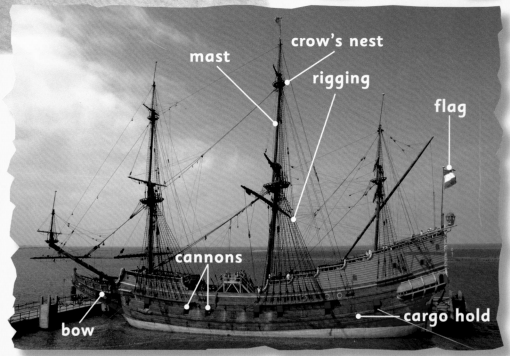

mast

crow's nest

rigging

flag

cannons

bow

cargo hold

What if ...

You are a ship builder. The mermaids have asked you to design a boat to travel both on the water and under the seas. It needs to be able to keep the water out and fight off sea monsters.

adjectives	verbs
antique	anchored
battered	attacked
damaged	capsized
gleaming	cast off
newly-painted	escaped
rusty	landed
shipshape	launched
speedy	navigated
strong	put to sea
sturdy	ran aground
swift	set sail
tattered	weighed anchor
wooden	
worn-out	

Treasure

Every pirate at sea is after one thing above all else — treasure!

nouns	adjectives
bullion	glittering
gold	glossy
hoard	glowing
jewels	golden
loot	lustrous
money	precious
prize	radiant
riches	shiny
silver	sparkling
	valuable

silver

doubloons

12

jewels

What if ...

You saw the pirates attack and steal the treasure. And from your hiding place you also saw them bury it in their secret hiding place. What do you do next?

gold bullion

coins

ONE OUNCE 9999 GOLD

Islands

Islands are surrounded by water. An island can be a great place for pirates to hide, especially if it has fresh water and lots of food.

Types of islands

An **archipelago** is a group of many islands.
An **atoll** is a coral island.
A **Caribbean key** is a very low lying island.
A **peninsula** isn't an island but it is a piece of land almost surrounded by water. It is connected to the mainland by a thin neck of land.

Is your island deserted or full of life?

adjectives

bare	lonely
breathtaking	marooned
dazzling	stunning
desolate	terrific
deserted	uninhabited
exciting	unusual
isolated	wonderful

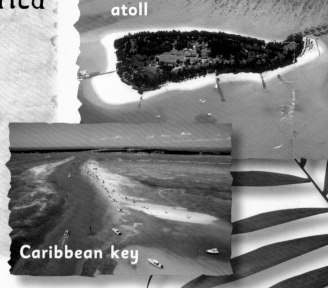

atoll

Caribbean key

14

archipelago

A fierce storm hits and the pirates need to pull into the closest harbor.

Types of storms

nouns

blizzard	monsoon
cloudburst	squall
cyclone	tornado
downpour	twister
hurricane	typhoon
lightning	

The island is covered in thick jungle and rocky peaks. How do you get about the island?

verbs

clamber	fight	sprint
claw	jog	struggle
climb	race	trek
crash	ride	walk
crawl	run	wander
dash	scramble	

15

Maps

Pirates needed maps of the lands and seas. They also used star maps to find their way at night. And, of course there were treasure maps to remember where the treasure was buried!

Map words

The main points on a **compass** are North, East, South, and West. An arrow marked on a map always points to north. A way to remember their order is: **N**ever **E**at **S**oggy **W**affles (clockwise).

Latitude and longitude are used to tell distance. Lines of latitude go around the globe like the Equator. Lines of longitude go up and down, north to south.

The scale tells us how to accurately measure distance, e.g., 1 centimeter on the map stands for 1 kilometer.

The legend explains the symbols used on the map.

Star maps show the sky at night. Sailors can use stars to tell direction at night.

17

The Seven Seas

There may once have been only seven seas but there are now many, many more. Oceans are larger than seas. In what waters will your pirates sail?

Oceans

Antarctic Ocean
Arctic Ocean
Atlantic Ocean
Indian Ocean
Pacific Ocean

Some of the World's Seas

Adriatic Sea
Aegean Sea
Arabian Sea
Arafura Sea
Baffin Bay
Bali Sea
Baltic Sea
Bay of Bengal

Bering Sea
Black Sea
Caribbean Sea
Caspian Sea
China Sea
Greenland Sea
Gulf of Alaska
Gulf of Mexico

Mediterranean Sea
Persian Gulf
Red Sea
Sargasso Sea
Sea of Japan
Tasman Sea
Timor sea

Can you find them all in the atlas?

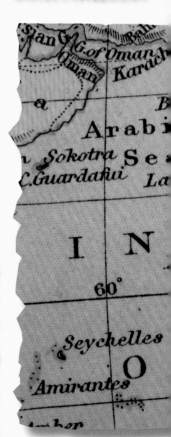

Red Sea

Baltic Sea

What does the sea look like?

adjectives

angry	rough
bumpy	stormy
calm	swirling
choppy	turbulent
dark	violent
murky	wild
raging	windswept

What color is the water?

aquamarine	midnight blue
azure	navy blue
blue green	sapphire
cyan	sea green
deep blue	teal
indigo	turquoise
emerald	ultramarine
marine	

Writing a Story

You are shipwrecked on a desert island without water.
You have to be rescued.
The only ship you see is a pirate ship.
What will you do now?

What is the pirate captain like?

What type of ship do the pirates have?

How will you get the pirates to
stop and pick you up?

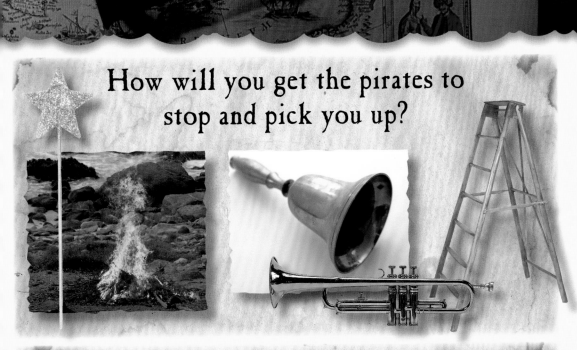

How can you make yourself useful to the pirates
so they don't make you walk the plank?

How does your story end?

21

Writing Nonfiction

Write a report about a science experiment. Science reports are factual — they tell about a real experiment that can be repeated by others.

What things float?

Hypothesis

What do you think will happen?
What types of materials do you think will float?

Materials
A list of the things that you will test.

Method
Write about what you did.

Results
What happened? What floated? What sank?
Draw a table.

Final statement

Write a short statement that tells us what you found out.

Glossary

bleached
color is faded to white

bombarded
attacked with heavy gunfire

boom
make a loud, deep sound

breeches
trousers reaching to just below
the knee

bullion
bars of gold or silver

felucca
a long narrow boat; oars are needed

galley
a kitchen on a boat

gunwales
the top edge of a boat's sides

legend
tells what symbols on a map mean

lustrous
glossy, shining, and bright

marauder
someone who raids and loots to
steal goods

marooned
left alone; abandoned

ruthless
very hard and cruel

schooner
a big sailing ship with two or
more masts

skiff
a small boat with sails or oars

squall
a brief, violent storm

turbulent
disturbed air or water that makes
sudden changes of direction

weigh anchor
pull the anchor in

whooped
shouted loudly in an excited way

zany
odd and funny